BEAUTICIANS TE[illegible] ALL

by

DENISE FOSTER-PATRICK

It's by God's Grace
Thank you!
"Mainy"

ISBN: 1-58597-123-5
LOC: 2001096726

Dedicated

With

"Forever love"

To my parents,

Fred & Henrietta Foster

ACKNOWLEDGMENT

To God, who is the Author and Finisher of my faith I praise you, even with this book of humor.

THANK YOU

To my girlfriends for support in the rough times: Crystal Harriel, Monya Kegler, Neressa Wilkins, Jeanette Ramsey, June Wayne "Pebbles"

Thank You

Marietta Washington, Fred Foster Jr.
(Sister & Brother role models are always cool.)

To Mrs. Sandy Goff for designing such a neat cover. Let Sandy know that you like her drawing abilities at: bySanD@att.net

Much love and respect goes to all of my beautician friends.

But a special thank you goes out to my first beautician:
Mrs. Deborah Davis who has been my inspiration down through the years and one of the funniest beauticians I know. Thanks for keeping it "real".
The thank you section wouldn't be complete until I mention a special "something, something" to my own fine boys: Marcus (age 6) & Jordan (age 3) thank you for all the extra hugs and kisses... now, go to bed!

Dear Ladies,
What would be the name of a book when you ask the most over worked, often criticized, unappreciated, professionals to tell you about their day?

<u>**Beauticians Tell All**</u>

It's a collection of humorous one liners told by our beloved; hairstylist, hairdresser, anointed hands, hook- you- up-Queens, Etc. (You name it)

As I was gathering facts for my book, I noticed a pattern among <u>all</u> women. It doesn't matter what color your skin is, or what type of hair you have, women are women.

We can be the sweetest, mild mannered creatures on the face of the earth until we have a

"Bad hair day".

Then the world better watch out! That of course, isn't an excuse to be rough on hairstylist.

(She is our fixer upper.)

This book is to make you laugh. And I guarantee you will see others in this, but if you happen to run across something you personally can identify with, I hope you can laugh at yourself, change your behavior, hug your fixer upper, and have a brand new appreciation for what they go through.

Now, sit back and enjoy <u>Beauticians Tell All.</u>

* Conduct Unbecoming
* Time Management
* Money Matters
* Say Hello, then Goodbye
* Do People Really Act Like This?
* Train Up Your Child
* Home Remedies
* A Day at the Salon

CONDUCT UNBECOMING

1. Customer expects their hair to look like model's hair in the stylebook.
When clearly model has thick hair or it's a weave and your customer has thin hair and doesn't want to buy more.

CONDUCT UNBECOMING

2. Customer has short hair with long hair taste.

3. Another beautician damages customer's hair and she expects you to cure her in one visit.

CONDUCT UNBECOMING

4. You have been doing hair for years and customers challenge your calling.

5. Customer's hair really looks good after you have worked so hard on it and suddenly it rains, but customer doesn't try to cover your <u>work</u>.

CONDUCT UNBECOMING

6. Customer tells you that they always tip waiters, but has never tipped you.

7. You had just cut customer's hair but next week they want a weave.

CONDUCT UNBECOMING

8. Customer uses time in chair as their therapy session and when you give your opinion they get an attitude.

9. Customer asks you to do style in hair book, but they complain afterwards.
(You knew it was going to be ugly!)

CONDUCT UNBECOMING

10. You wipe behind customer's ears, and your towel will never be the same.

11. Customer keeps bringing her dog to the salon.

CONDUCT UNBECOMING

12. The customer got wet when "they" moved while at the wash bowl.
    (Now they have an attitude with you.)

13. Customer brings friend along so you can work her in, which causes you to be behind the whole day.

CONDUCT UNBECOMING

14. Customer takes comb and rearranges hair and now it's ugly.
(And you know she is going to tell everybody who did her hair.)

15. Customer gets up several times while under the dryer to go to the restroom, talk to other customers and wonders why it's taking so long for her hair to dry.
(She swears something is wrong with the dryer)

Time Management

1. Customer shows up for appointment later than 10 minutes without calling.

2. Customer is a no show, and you just turned someone else away because you were booked solid for the day.

Time Management

3. Customer shows up late for appointment and has an attitude about waiting.

4. No show customer calls to reschedule, but the time she wants in is not available and she gets an attitude. (But you didn't cause any of this)

Time Management

5. Customer complains about always leaving in the dark but continues to make night or evening appointments.

6. Customer rushes in your salon an hour before her wedding begins.

Money Matters

1. Your so-called friend wants credit.

2. First time customer bounces check.

Money Matters

3. Customer argues about paying bank fee for bouncing check.

4. Customer asks if you will take her food stamps as your payment.

Money Matters

5. Customer pays you with change.
   (And said "you got paid didn't you, it all spends")

6. Customer wants to set up a payment plan for services rendered.

Money Matters

7. Customer bounced check once and when told about it she got an attitude with you for mentioning it.

8. Your" friend" has written you 2 bad checks and when you explain no more checks she doesn't understand why.

Money Matters

9. Customer doesn't have enough money and makes a scene in the salon with you to pay next week.

10. Same customer just told you earlier about her going to a shoe sale tomorrow.

Money Matters

11. You unknowingly accept counterfeit money.

12. Police show up in your salon asking you all sorts of questions, now your salon is under surveillance.

13. Customer wants you to mail her your bill. She will need at least 30 days to pay you.

SAY HELLO, THEN GOODBYE, PLEASE!

1. Customer has long winded conversation on your telephone.

2. Customer figured out how to make long distance calls on your phone with the block on it.
(The Phone Company still wants you to pay)

SAY HELLO, THEN GOODBYE, PLEASE!

3. Customer dial 1-900 #'s from your phone.
   (Before you blocked it)

4. Customer accepted a collect call on your phone from "<u>June bug</u>". (On Lock down)

SAY HELLO, THEN GOODBYE, PLEASE!

5. Customer gives salon number as callback number without your permission.

6. Customer talks too loud on the phone.

SAY HELLO, THEN GOODBYE, PLEASE!

7. Customer uses profanity while on the phone and it bothers other customers.

8. Customer was on cell phone, but should have been under the dryer, and wonders why her hair isn't dry.

SAY HELLO, THEN GOODBYE, PLEASE!

9. Customer's pager goes off constantly and it's the very irritating kind.

10. Customer ignores the 3-minute limit sign over the phone.

SAY HELLO, THEN GOODBYE, PLEASE!

11. Customer gets upset with person on the phone and slams the receiver down and breaks the base.

12. Customer answers salon's phone with an attitude chewing gum, and yells for that person to pick up.

DO PEOPLE REALLY ACT LIKE THIS?

1. "No Smoking" signs up all over the place, yet customer smokes anyway.

2. No smoking signs are up but your friend asks you can they take 2 quick drags.

DO PEOPLE REALLY ACT LIKE THIS?

3. Customer waiting to be serviced says something negative about customer's hair you are currently working on.

4. Customer comes in with big dinner items: chicken, green beans, mashed potatoes (you get the picture) and don't even offer you <u>the juice.</u>

DO PEOPLE REALLY ACT LIKE THIS?

5. Customer steals hair style books.

6. Customer steals curlers.

DO PEOPLE REALLY ACT LIKE THIS?

7. Customer drops potato chips on the floor and doesn't offer to clean them up.

8. Customer can't get along with anyone in the salon.

DO PEOPLE REALLY ACT LIKE THIS?

9. Customer always criticizes the shop's location.
   (Although she passed by 5 others before reaching yours)
   <u>**Hint! Hint!**</u>

10. Customer criticizes the parking.

DO PEOPLE REALLY ACT LIKE THIS?

11. Customer complains about "your" days <u>off</u>.

12. Customer says she borrowed your magazine for the <u>recipes</u>, but didn't ask you for permission.

DO PEOPLE REALLY ACT LIKE THIS?

13. Customer thinks she knows everybody's business and spreads it all over the salon.

14. Customer breaks something in the salon and doesn't offer to pay for it, or says <u>"It wasn't me."</u>

DO PEOPLE REALLY ACT LIKE THIS?

15. Customer moves things around in "your" salon. (As though they are redecorating).

16. Customer comes in drunk and high, and wants you to make them look <u>good.</u>

DO PEOPLE REALLY ACT LIKE THIS?

17. Customers breath stinks and they won't take a mint.
(You're not sure what's worst the breath or the chemicals)

18. Customer fights with another customer.

DO PEOPLE REALLY ACT LIKE THIS?

19. Customer at every appointment is always trying to get you to join what you know is a network-marketing scheme.

20. Customer takes shoes off and stinks up the place.
(Smells like corn chips and vinegar)

DO PEOPLE REALLY ACT LIKE THIS?

21. Customer snores under the dryer and rocks the salon. (The little kids get scared)

22. Same customer falls out the seat.

DO PEOPLE REALLY ACT LIKE THIS?

23. Customer changes channel on your TV.
(Without your permission.)

24. Customer talks during your favorite soap opera.

DO PEOPLE REALLY ACT LIKE THIS?

25. Customer sings wrong words during your favorite song.

26. Customer complains about prices to others customers right in front of you.

DO PEOPLE REALLY ACT LIKE THIS?

27. Customer expects a Christmas gift.

28. Customer leaves belongings in the shop for weeks and when you decide to throw those items away, customer comes back in asking for them.

DO PEOPLE REALLY ACT LIKE THIS?

29. Customer steals this book!

DO PEOPLE REALLY ACT LIKE THIS?

30. Customer comes to salon and sleeps every time. (It would be nice to have a little conversation.)

31. As you wash your customer's hair you notice that under your fingernails are getting pretty dirty.

DO PEOPLE REALLY ACT LIKE THIS?

32. Customer leaves the salon not realizing she is still wearing the cape.

33. Customer comes in running and panting because the police are after her.

DO PEOPLE REALLY ACT LIKE THIS?

34. Customer uses a toothbrush to style her baby hair.

35. Customer refuses to cut side burns.
(And she's beginning to look a lot like Elvis)

DO PEOPLE REALLY ACT LIKE THIS?

36. Customer wants you to cut her boyfriend's name in her head.

37. Customer wears house shoes to the salon.
(The big furry kind)

DO PEOPLE REALLY ACT LIKE THIS?

38. Customer goes on a talk show and complains about you and your salon.

39. Your current boyfriend picks up that lady you just met in the salon.

40. Customer wants to use your salon to sale hot stuff. (But she calls it lukewarm stuff)

TRAIN UP YOUR CHILD

1. Parent can't control their children in the salon.

2. This is the same parent always giving advice to other customers about raising children.

TRAIN UP YOUR CHILD

3. Child won't sit still in the chair and mom gets an attitude with you.

4. Child always wants to eat while getting hair done.

TRAIN UP YOUR CHILD

5. Child's ride is always late and you begin to feel like you are running a day care.

6. Child plays the spinning game in your chair.

TRAIN UP YOUR CHILD

7. Child has a bad attitude with or without parent being there.

8. While pressing child's hair she jumps, you burn her ear and parent gets upset with you.

TRAIN UP YOUR CHILD

9. Father comes in complaining about daughter's hair, but he has combed her hair only once. (And that's when she was a baby... she's six now)

10. Child raises head up while at the wash bowl and gets you wet.

11. Customer leaves dirty diaper in the restroom.

TRAIN UP YOUR CHILD

12. Child's hair has lice.

13. Child waiting to be serviced gets into fight with child waiting for mom and the first child leaves.

    (And there goes dollar signs)

14. Bottom line is this: YOU DON'T TAKE YOUR MISBEHAVED, UNDISCIPLINED CHILDREN TO YOUR JOB, SO DON'T BRING THEM TO MINE. MY JOB IS JUST AS IMPORTANT AS YOURS IS.

HOME REMEDIES

1. Customer is too cheap to pay for quality home hair care products.
   (And wonders why her hair is not healthy).

2. Customer didn't tell you everything she did to her hair and then what you do turns her hair green.

HOME REMEDIES

3. Customer uses rubber bands on hair and wonders why there is breakage.

4. Customer scratches scalp day before chemicals are to be applied, next day scalp burns and she has attitude with you.

HOME REMEDIES

5. Customer washes hair with dishwashing soap.

6. Customer uses hot curlers everyday but lies to you about doing it, and expects you to condition and repair it for free.

HOME REMEDIES

7. Customer still wants scalp greased instead of oiled. (Over age 30 will get this one)

8. Customer uses beer to wash hair.
(Because of the foam)

HOME REMEDIES

9. Customer asks her friend to give her a perm and hair begins to shed and wants you "The professional" to fix it.

(She should have gone to "the professional" in the first place.)

HOME REMEDIES

10. Customer only deals with stylists who are still in training to get cheaper prices.

11. Customer thinks she has <u>culturally</u> different hair.

HOME REMEDIES

12. Customer adds water to shampoo to stretch it, and wonders why it's not really clean or itch free.

13. Customer believes that baby oil and water will make her hair curly.

14. Customer put her own weave in but you can see the track and clumps of glue.

A DAY AT THE SALON

1. Stylist next to you criticizes the customer's hair you are working on, takes over without your permission and your customer starts going to her.

2. Stylist next to you runs out of products and always want to *borrow* yours.

A DAY AT THE SALON

3. Stylist tells other people it's ok to sit in your chair instead of asking them to sit in the waiting area.

4. You wonder why the television and music are on at the same time.

A DAY AT THE SALON

5. Stylist next to you comes to work late <u>all</u> the time.

6. Stylist works too fast and customer hair doesn't look good.

A DAY AT THE SALON

7. Stylist works too slow every strand of hair is locked into place, but her other customers are backing up.

A DAY AT THE SALON

8. Shampoo girl rubs head too soft.
(Just enough to irritate you)

9. Shampoo girl rubs head too hard.
(You ask her if she left any skin up there)

A DAY AT THE SALON

10. You see so much dandruff in customer's head you recommend them to see a doctor before coming back *"up in here".*

A DAY AT THE SALON

11. You see male stylist charging an extra $15.00 for his services, but he always blows kisses to his customers.

12. Stylist overbooks appointments and complains about being tired.

A DAY AT THE SALON

13. Stylist next to you refuses to believe that the "No Smoking" sign includes her.

14. You realize you are doing a customer's hair that is being featured on <u>America's Most Wanted.</u>

A DAY AT THE SALON

15. Stylist next to you takes too many walk ins and you have been waiting for your next customer for over 30 minutes.

16. You have been standing all day and your feet hurt and nobody seems to care.

A DAY AT THE SALON

17. Your license picture looks like a mug shot instead of a glamour shot.

18. Stylist next to you doesn't sweep hair up off the floor and other customers think that you did it.

A DAY AT THE SALON

19. You have been working hard all day and look in the mirror and realize your hair is a mess.
(But you don't care)

20. At the end of a crazy day you look up toward heaven and say, God I want to thank you
for yet another day.

Tidbit's about the Author

Denise Foster-Patrick a woman who is truly redefining herself. Not by herself however, she is looking to the only True Wise God through her Lord and Savior Jesus Christ and because of the Holy Spirit leading and His guidance she's got purpose and meaning like never before.

(Her ultimate fixer upper)

She is her kid's mom, a keynote speaker, and a CEO. (Chief Encouragement Officer)

Want to tell your story for the next project?

Write to: Beauticians TELL ALL
Attn: Denise Foster-Patrick
14310 E. 42nd St. # 295
INDEPENDENCE, MO 64055
Email: Dapat1@msn.com
Vmail: Kansas & Missouri: 816-830-7653
Out of area: 1-800-677-2357 # 07
Knee mail: Proverbs 3: 4-7